A great motivator once said that...

> "A total commitment is
> paramount to reaching the
> ultimate in performance."

This collection of quotations has been
compiled to inspire us all to reach
for life's greatest achievements.

"Every job is a self-portrait of the person who did it. Autograph your work with excellence."

"Quality is never an accident; it is always the result of high intention, sincere effort, intelligent direction and skillful execution; it represents the wise choice of many alternatives."

Willa A. Foster

"The difference between failure and success is doing a thing nearly right and doing a thing exactly right."

Edward Simmons

"Desire is the key to motivation, but it's the determination and commitment to an unrelenting pursuit of your goal—a commitment to excellence—that will enable you to attain the success you seek."

Mario Andretti
Race Car Driver

"If better is possible,
 Good is not enough."

"Do not wish to be anything but what you are, and try to be that perfectly."

St. Francis De Sales

"Some men dream of worthy accomplishments, while others stay awake and do them."

"To dream anything that you want to dream. That is the beauty of the human mind. To do anything that you want to do. That is the strength of the human will. To trust yourself to test your limits. That is the courage to succeed."

Bernard Edmonds
American Writer

"All glory comes from daring to begin."

Eugene F. Ware
American Lawyer/Poet

"We are what we repeatedly do. Excellence, then, is not an act but a habit."

Planning for a 30 yr retirmet reguires a ~~contrat~~ continual commitat to exallne.

~~best ever~~

we can help!
Let's chat!

"Well done is better than well said."

Ben Franklin

"Unless you try to do something beyond what you have already mastered, you will never grow."

Ronald E. Osborn

"The ultimate victory in competition is derived from the inner satisfaction of knowing that you have done your best and that you have gotten the most out of what you had to give."

Howard Cosell
Sports Broadcaster

"Many of life's failures are men who did not realize how close they were to success when they gave up."

"I am a big believer in the 'mirror test'. All that matters is if you can look in the mirror and honestly tell the person you see there, that you've done your best."

John McKay
NFL Coach

"Do not follow where the path may lead. Go instead where there is no path and leave a trail."

"When we have done our best,
we should wait the result in
peace."

J. Lubbock

"Some men see things as they are and say 'Why?' I dream things that never were, and say, 'Why not'?"

George Bernard Shaw

"When we have done our best, we should wait the result in peace."

J. Lubbock

"Some men see things as they are and say 'Why?' I dream things that never were, and say, 'Why not'?"

George Bernard Shaw

C18

"It's what you learn after you
know it all that counts."

John Wooden

"A winner is someone who sets his goals, commits himself to those goals, and then pursues his goals with all the ability given him."

Lets us help your reach your retirement goals

Lts. chat

we can help

"If a man is called to be a streetsweeper, he should sweep streets even as Michelangelo painted, or Beethoven composed music, or Shakespeare wrote poetry. He should sweep streets so well that all the hosts of heaven and earth will pause to say, here lived a great streetsweeper who did his job well."

Martin Luther King, Jr.

our retirement lifestyle plans make Michelangelo jealous!

E.g. Planning 20 yr. retirements is fraught w/ Risk —

C21

"A total commitment is paramount to reaching the ultimate in performance."

Tom Flores
NFL Coach

we are committed
to your success

C22

"The price of success is hard work, dedication to the job at hand, and the determination that whether we win or lose, we have applied the best of ourselves to the task at hand."

Vince Lombardi
NFL Coach

"The greatest thing in this
world is not so much where
we are, but in what direction
we are moving."

O.W. Holmes

C24

"No one ever attains very eminent success by simply doing what is required of him; it is the amount and excellence of what is over and above the required, that determines the greatness of ultimate distinction."

Charles Kendall Adams

our retirement lifestyle
Plans go above &
Beyond -

we FIX Broken retirement
Plans -

"The spirit, the will to win, and the will to excel are the things that endure. These qualities are so much more important than the events that occur."

Vince Lombardi
NFL Coach

"There are four steps to accomplishment: Plan Purposefully. Prepare Prayerfully. Proceed Positively. Pursue Persistently."

"Only those who dare to fail greatly can ever achieve greatly."

"One man has enthusiasm for 30 minutes, another for 30 days, but it is the man who has it for 30 years who makes a success of his life."

Edward B. Butler
American Scientist

"The secret of success in life is for a man to be ready for his opportunity when it comes."

Benjamin Disraeli

"I do the best I know how, the very best I can; and I mean to keep on doing it to the end. If the end brings me out all right, what is said against me will not amount to anything. If the end brings me out all wrong, ten angels swearing I was right would make no difference."

Abraham Lincoln

"People forget how fast you
  did a job—but they remember
  how well you did it."

"One of life's most painful moments comes when we must admit that we didn't do our homework, that we are not prepared."

Merlin Olsen
NFL Tackle, Sports Broadcaster/Actor

2nd opinion

C33

"Never, Never, Never Quit."

Winston Churchill

"If you don't invest very much, then defeat doesn't hurt very much and winning is not very exciting."

Dick Vermeil
NFL Coach

"Choice, not chance, determines destiny."

right reverent Liberty
Pior

"I always view problems as opportunities in work clothes."

Henry Kaiser

"When an archer misses the mark, he turns and looks for the fault within himself. Failure to hit the bull's-eye is never the fault of the target. To improve your aim—improve yourself."

Gilbert Arland

Our retirement lifestyle Plans will improve your life n retirement.

Let's chat

"Good is not good
where better is
expected."

Thomas Fuller

> "Our chief want in life is somebody who will make us do what we can."
>
> **Ralph Waldo Emerson**

Protect your lifestyle
for the rest of
your lives

"You will become as small as your controlling desire; as great as your dominant aspiration."

James Allen

> **"To succeed—do the best you can, where you are, with what you have."**

Taxes are the single
BIGGEST EXPENSE in our
lives

~~our tax~~ quote

— Testament —

Let's chat

C42

"Men are often capable of greater things than they perform. They are sent into the world with bills of credit, and seldom draw to their full extent."

Walpole

"Winning isn't everything—it's the only thing."

Vince Lombardi

"The difference between the impossible and the possible lies in a man's determination."

Tommy Lasorda
Major League Manager

X

"A great pleasure in life is doing what people say you cannot do."

Walter Gagehot

"Ingenuity, plus courage, plus work, equals miracles."

Bob Richards
Pole Vaulter
Two time Olympic Gold Medalist

"The road to success is paved with good intentions."

"If you've made up your mind you can do something, you're absolutely right."

"Do not let what you cannot do interfere with what you can do."

John Wooden
College Basketball Coach

"Real leaders are ordinary people with extraordinary determination."

"Enthusiasm is the propelling force necessary for climbing the ladder of success."

"We cannot direct the wind...But we can adjust the sails."

"Don't measure yourself
by what you have
accomplished, but by
what you should have
accomplished with your
ability."

"Failure is not the worst thing
in the world. The very worst
is not to try."

"The harder you work
the luckier you get."

Gary Player
Golfer

"The only time you can't afford to fail is the last time you try."

Charles Kettering

Retirement

You only get one chance
to sub it right.

"Hope sees the invisible, feels the intangible and achieves the impossible."

"Great minds must be ready not only to take opportunities, but to make them."

Colton

"The man who cannot believe in himself cannot believe in anything else."

Roy L. Smith
American Clergyman

✓ ✓

> "Today's preparation
> determines tomorrow's
> achievement."

Planning for a 30yr.
retirement is full of Risk —

LETS US . . . . —

"Act as though it were impossible to fail."

"The man who goes farthest is generally the one who is willing to do and dare. The sure-thing boat never gets far from shore."

Dale Carnegie
American Author

"The quality of a person's life is in direct proportion to their commitment to excellence, regardless of their chosen field of endeavor."

Vincent T. Lombardi

"It takes courage to push yourself to places that you have never been before...to test your limits...to break through barriers."

"There is always room
at the top."

Daniel Webster

"Don't be afraid to take a big step if one is indicated. You can't cross a chasm in two small jumps."

David Lloyd George
Former Prime Minister of England

"He is great who can do what he wishes; he is wise who wishes to do what he can."

"Nothing great will ever be achieved without great men, and men are great only if they are determined to be so."

Charles de Gaulle

"Accept the challenges, so that you may feel the exhilaration of victory."

General George S. Patton

25 RISKS -
   challenges .

"People seldom improve when they have no other model but themselves to copy after."

Goldsmith

"The difference between ordinary and extraordinary is that little extra." —

[handwritten notes:]

TSull...

... EXTraordinary

written by Kellington

TESTAMMAL

Call to action

"Paralyze resistance with persistence."

Woody Hayes
College Football Coach

"It's a funny thing about life: If you refuse to accept anything but the very best you will very often get it."

W. Somerset Maugham

Best life ever

Order Your Favorite Quote Today!

Timeless... Your favorite quote on a beautiful brass plate mounted on a walnut finished base. A real conversation piece for your home or office.

"**T**he quality of a Person's life is In direct proportion To their commitment To excellence, Regardless of their Chosen field of Endeavor."

PRICE LIST

	BRASS PLAQUE
	Beautiful brass plate mounted on walnut finished base. Outside dimensions - 8 x 10.
1	**$25.00**
2-10	**$19.00**
11-25	**$17.00**

Over 25: please call for custom quote.

Shipping and handling:
Add $3.00 per unit on quantities of 1-10.
Add $2.50 per unit on quantities of 11-25.

MAIL ORDER FORM TO:

GREAT QUOTATIONS, INC.
919 SPRINGER DRIVE•LOMBARD, IL 60148-6416

TOLL FREE: 800-621-1432 (outside Illinois)
(708) 953-1222

ORDER FORM

QTY	PRODUCT	QUOTE PAGE NUMBER	UNIT PRICE	TOTAL PRICE

MAIL ORDER FORM TO:

GREAT QUOTATIONS, INC.
919 Springer Drive
Lombard, Illinois 60148-6416
Local (708) 953-1222
Toll-Free 800-621-1432

SUBTOTAL	$
6 ¼ % SALES TAX (IL RES.)	$
SHIPPING & HANDLING	$
TOTAL	$

NAME _____

ADDRESS _____

CITY_____ **STATE**_____ **ZIP**_____

Phone Number ( ) _____

Enclosed is my check or money order for $ made
out to Great Quotations, Inc.

Charge my ☐ VISA   ☐ MASTER CARD

Card Number_____Exp. date_____

Signature _____

Other Great Quotations Books:

- Happle Birthday
- Best of Success
- Great Quotes/
  Great Leaders
- Aged to Perfection
- Retirement
- Love on Your
  Wedding...
- Thank You
- Thinking of You
- Words of Love
- Words for Friendship
- To My Love
- Inspirations
- Sports Quotes

- Never Never Quit
- Motivational Quotes
- Customer Care
- Commitment to
  Quaity
- Over the Hill
- Golf Humor
- Happy Birthday
  to the Golfer
- Handle Stress
- Great Quotes/
  Great Women
- A smiles increases
  your face Value
- Keys to Happiness
- Things you'll learn...

GREAT QUOTATIONS, INC.
919 SPRINGER DRIVE • LOMBARD, IL 60148 - 6416

TOLL FREE: 800-621-1432 (Outside Illinois)
(708) 953-1222

PRINTED IN HONG KONG